NORTH CAROLINA RULE
2018 Edition

Updated through January 1, 2018

I0053061

Michigan Legal Publishing Ltd.
QUICK DESK REFERENCE SERIES™

Academic and bulk discounts available at
www.michlp.com

WE WELCOME YOUR FEEDBACK: info@michlp.com

ISBN-13: 978-1-64002-039-9

Table of Contents

§ 8C-1. Rules of Evidence.

The North Carolina Rules of Evidence are as follows:

Article 1. General Provisions.

Rule 101. Scope.

These rules govern proceedings in the courts of this State to the extent and with the exceptions stated in Rule 1101.

Rule 102. Purpose and construction.

(a) **In general**. - These rules shall be construed to secure fairness in administration, elimination of unjustifiable expense and delay, and promotion of growth and development of the law of evidence to the end that the truth may be ascertained and proceedings justly determined.

(b) **Subordinate divisions**. - For the purpose of these rules only, the subordinate division of any rule which is labeled with a lower case letter shall be a subdivision.

Rule 103. Rulings on evidence.

(a) **Effect of erroneous ruling**. - Error may not be predicated upon a ruling which admits or excludes evidence unless a substantial right of the party is affected, and

   (1) *Objection*. - In case the ruling is one admitting evidence, a timely objection or motion to strike appears of record. No particular form is required in order to preserve the right to assert the alleged error upon appeal if the motion or objection clearly presented the alleged error to the trial court;

   (2) *Offer of proof*. - In case the ruling is one excluding evidence, the substance of the evidence was made known to the court by offer or was apparent from the context within which questions were asked.

Once the court makes a definitive ruling on the record admitting or excluding evidence, either at or before trial, a party need not renew an objection or offer of proof to preserve a claim of error for appeal.

(b) **Record of offer and ruling**. - The court may add any other or further statement which shows the character of the evidence, the form in which it was offered, the objection made, and the ruling thereon. It may direct the making of an offer in question and answer form.

(c) **Hearing of jury**. - In jury cases, proceedings shall be conducted, to the extent practicable, so as to prevent inadmissible evidence from being suggested to the jury by any means, such as making statements or offers of proof or asking questions in the hearing of the jury.

(d) **Review of errors where justice requires**. - Notwithstanding the requirements of subdivision (a) of this rule, an appellate court may review errors affecting substantial rights if it determines, in the interest of justice, it is appropriate to do so.

Rule 104. Preliminary questions.

(a) **Questions of admissibility generally**. - Preliminary questions concerning the qualification of a person to be a witness, the existence of a privilege, or the admissibility of evidence shall be determined by the court, subject to the provisions of subdivision (b). In making its determination it is not bound by the rules of evidence except those with respect to privileges.

(b) **Relevancy conditioned on fact**. - When the relevancy of evidence depends upon the fulfillment of a condition of fact, the court shall admit it upon, or subject to, the introduction of evidence sufficient to support a finding of the fulfillment of the condition.

(c) **Hearing of jury**. - Hearings on the admissibility of confessions or other motions to suppress evidence in criminal trials in Superior Court shall in all cases be conducted out of the hearing of the jury. Hearings on other preliminary matters shall be so conducted when the interests of justice require or, when an accused is a witness, if he so requests.

(d) **Testimony by accused**. - The accused does not, by testifying upon a preliminary matter, subject himself to cross-examination as to other issues in the case.

(e) **Weight and credibility**. - This rule does not limit the right of a party to introduce before the jury evidence relevant to weight or credibility.

Rule 105. Limited admissibility.

When evidence which is admissible as to one party or for one purpose but not admissible as to another party or for another purpose is admitted, the court, upon request, shall restrict the evidence to its proper scope and instruct the jury accordingly.

Rule 106. Remainder of or related writings or recorded statements.

When a writing or recorded statement or part thereof is introduced by a party, an adverse party may require him at that time to introduce any other part or any other writing or recorded statement which ought in fairness to be considered contemporaneously with it.

Article 2. Judicial Notice.

Rule 201. Judicial notice of adjudicative facts.

(a) **Scope of rule**. - This rule governs only judicial notice of adjudicative facts.

(b) **Kinds of facts**. - A judicially noticed fact must be one not subject to reasonable dispute in that it is either (1) generally known within the territorial jurisdiction of the trial court or (2) capable of accurate and ready determination by resort to sources whose accuracy cannot reasonably be questioned.

(c) **When discretionary**. - A court may take judicial notice, whether requested or not.

(d) **When mandatory**. - A court shall take judicial notice if requested by a party and supplied with the necessary information.

(e) **Opportunity to be heard**. - In a trial court, a party is entitled upon timely request to an opportunity to be heard as to the propriety of taking judicial notice and the tenor of the matter noticed. In the absence of prior notification, the request may be made after judicial notice has been taken.

(f) **Time of taking notice**. - Judicial notice may be taken at any stage of the proceeding.

(g) **Instructing jury**. - In a civil action or proceeding, the court shall instruct the jury to accept as conclusive any fact judicially noticed. In a criminal case, the court shall instruct the jury that it may, but is not required to, accept as conclusive any fact judicially noticed.

Article 3. Presumptions in Civil Actions and Proceedings.

Rule 301. Presumptions in general in civil actions and proceedings.

In all civil actions and proceedings when not otherwise provided for by statute, by judicial decision, or by these rules, a presumption imposes on the party against whom it is directed the burden of going forward with evidence to rebut or meet the presumption, but does not shift to such party the burden of proof in the sense of the risk of nonpersuasion, which remains throughout the trial upon the party on whom it was originally cast. The burden of going forward is satisfied by the introduction of evidence sufficient to permit reasonable minds to conclude that the presumed fact does not exist. If the party against whom a presumption operates fails to meet the burden of producing evidence, the presumed fact shall be deemed proved, and the court shall instruct the jury accordingly. When the burden of producing evidence to meet a presumption is satisfied, the court must instruct the jury that it may, but is not required to, infer the existence of the presumed fact from the proved fact.

Rule 302. Applicability of federal law in civil actions and proceedings.

In civil actions and proceedings, the effect of a presumption respecting a fact which is an element of a claim or defense as to which federal law supplies the rule of decision is determined in accordance with federal law.

Article 4. Relevancy and Its Limits.

Rule 401. Definition of "relevant evidence."

"Relevant evidence" means evidence having any tendency to make the existence of any fact that is of consequence to the determination of the action more probable or less probable than it would be without the evidence.

Rule 402. Relevant evidence generally admissible; irrelevant evidence inadmissible.

All relevant evidence is admissible, except as otherwise provided by the Constitution of the United States, by the Constitution of North Carolina, by Act of Congress, by Act of the General Assembly or by these rules. Evidence which is not relevant is not admissible.

Rule 403. Exclusion of relevant evidence on grounds of prejudice, confusion, or waste of time.

Although relevant, evidence may be excluded if its probative value is substantially outweighed by the danger of unfair prejudice, confusion of the issues, or misleading the jury, or by considerations of undue delay, waste of time, or needless presentation of cumulative evidence.

Rule 404. Character evidence not admissible to prove conduct; exceptions; other crimes.

(a) **Character evidence generally**. - Evidence of a person's character or a trait of his character is not admissible for the purpose of proving that he acted in conformity therewith on a particular occasion, except:

  (1) *Character of accused*. - Evidence of a pertinent trait of his character offered by an accused, or by the prosecution to rebut the same;

  (2) *Character of victim*. - Evidence of a pertinent trait of character of the victim of the crime offered by an accused, or by the prosecution to rebut the same, or evidence of a character trait of peacefulness of the victim offered by the prosecution in a homicide case to rebut evidence that the victim was the first aggressor;

  (3) *Character of witness*. - Evidence of the character of a witness, as provided in Rules 607, 608, and 609.

(b) **Other crimes, wrongs, or acts**. - Evidence of other crimes, wrongs, or acts is not admissible to prove the character of a person in order to show that he acted in conformity therewith. It may, however, be admissible for other purposes, such as proof of motive, opportunity, intent, preparation, plan, knowledge, identity, or absence of mistake, entrapment or accident. Admissible evidence may include evidence of an offense committed by a juvenile if it would have been a Class A, B1, B2, C, D, or E felony if committed by an adult.

Rule 405. Methods of proving character.

(a) **Reputation or opinion**. - In all cases in which evidence of character or a trait of character of a person is admissible, proof may be made by testimony as to reputation or by testimony in the form of an opinion. On cross-examination, inquiry is allowable into relevant specific instances of conduct. Expert testimony on character or a trait of character is not admissible as circumstantial evidence of behavior.

(b) **Specific instances of conduct**. - In cases in which character or a trait of character of a person is an essential element of a charge, claim, or defense, proof may also be made of specific instances of his conduct.

Rule 406. Habit; routine practice.

Evidence of the habit of a person or of the routine practice of an organization, whether corroborated or not and regardless of the presence of eyewitnesses, is relevant to prove that the conduct of the person or organization on a particular occasion was in conformity with the habit or routine practice.

Rule 407. Subsequent remedial measures.

When, after an event, measures are taken which, if taken previously, would have made the event less likely to occur, evidence of the subsequent measures is not admissible to prove negligence or culpable conduct in connection with the event. This rule does not require the exclusion of evidence of subsequent measures when offered for another purpose, such as proving ownership, control, or feasibility of precautionary measures, if those issues are controverted, or impeachment.

Rule 408. Compromise and offers to compromise.

Evidence of (1) furnishing or offering or promising to furnish, or (2) accepting or offering or promising to accept, a valuable consideration in compromising or attempting to compromise a claim which was disputed as to either validity or amount, is not admissible to prove liability for or invalidity of the claim or its amount. Evidence of conduct or evidence of statements made in compromise negotiations is likewise not admissible. This rule does not require the exclusion of any evidence otherwise discoverable merely because it is presented in the course of compromise negotiations. This rule also does not require exclusion when the evidence is offered for another purpose, such as proving bias or prejudice of a witness, negativing a contention of undue delay, or proving an effort to obstruct a criminal investigation or prosecution.

Rule 409. Payment of medical and other expenses.

Evidence of furnishing or offering or promising to pay medical, hospital, or other expenses occasioned by an injury is not admissible to prove liability for the injury.

Rule 410. Inadmissibility of pleas, plea discussions, and related statements.

Except as otherwise provided in this rule, evidence of the following is not, in any civil or criminal proceeding, admissible for or against the defendant who made the plea or was a participant in the plea discussions:
   (1) A plea of guilty which was later withdrawn;
   (2) A plea of no contest;

(3) Any statement made in the course of any proceedings under Article 58 of Chapter 15A of the General Statutes or comparable procedure in district court, or proceedings under Rule 11 of the Federal Rules of Criminal Procedure or comparable procedure in another state, regarding a plea of guilty which was later withdrawn or a plea of no contest;

(4) Any statement made in the course of plea discussions with an attorney for the prosecuting authority which do not result in a plea of guilty or which result in a plea of guilty later withdrawn.

However, such a statement is admissible in any proceeding wherein another statement made in the course of the same plea or plea discussions has been introduced and the statement ought in fairness be considered contemporaneously with it.

Rule 411. Liability insurance.

Evidence that a person was or was not insured against liability is not admissible upon the issue whether he acted negligently or otherwise wrongfully. This rule does not require the exclusion of evidence of insurance against liability when offered for another purpose, such as proof of agency, ownership, or control, or bias or prejudice of a witness.

Rule 412. Rape or sex offense cases; relevance of victim's past behavior.

(a) As used in this rule, the term "sexual behavior" means sexual activity of the complainant other than the sexual act which is at issue in the indictment on trial.

(b) Notwithstanding any other provision of law, the sexual behavior of the complainant is irrelevant to any issue in the prosecution unless such behavior:
(1) Was between the complainant and the defendant; or
(2) Is evidence of specific instances of sexual behavior offered for the purpose of showing that the act or acts charged were not committed by the defendant; or
(3) Is evidence of a pattern of sexual behavior so distinctive and so closely resembling the defendant's version of the alleged encounter with the complainant as to tend to prove that such complainant consented to the act or acts charged or behaved in such a manner as to lead the defendant reasonably to believe that the complainant consented; or
(4) Is evidence of sexual behavior offered as the basis of expert psychological or psychiatric opinion that the complainant fantasized or invented the act or acts charged.

(c) Sexual behavior otherwise admissible under this rule may not be proved by reputation or opinion.

(d) Notwithstanding any other provision of law, unless and until the court determines that evidence of sexual behavior is relevant under subdivision (b), no reference to this behavior may be made in the presence of the jury and no evidence of this behavior may be introduced at any time during the trial of:

    (1) A charge of rape or a lesser included offense of rape;

    (2) A charge of a sex offense or a lesser included offense of a sex offense; or

    (3) An offense being tried jointly with a charge of rape or a sex offense, or with a lesser included offense of rape or a sex offense.

Before any questions pertaining to such evidence are asked of any witness, the proponent of such evidence shall first apply to the court for a determination of the relevance of the sexual behavior to which it relates. The proponent of such evidence may make application either prior to trial pursuant to G.S. 15A-952, or during the trial at the time when the proponent desires to introduce such evidence. When application is made, the court shall conduct an in camera hearing, which shall be transcribed, to consider the proponent's offer of proof and the argument of counsel, including any counsel for the complainant, to determine the extent to which such behavior is relevant. In the hearing, the proponent of the evidence shall establish the basis of admissibility of such evidence. Notwithstanding subdivision (b) of Rule 104, if the relevancy of the evidence which the proponent seeks to offer in the trial depends upon the fulfillment of a condition of fact, the court, at the in camera hearing or at a subsequent in camera hearing scheduled for that purpose, shall accept evidence on the issue of whether that condition of fact is fulfilled and shall determine that issue. If the court finds that the evidence is relevant, it shall enter an order stating that the evidence may be admitted and the nature of the questions which will be permitted.

(e) The record of the in camera hearing and all evidence relating thereto shall be open to inspection only by the parties, the complainant, their attorneys and the court and its agents, and shall be used only as necessary for appellate review. At any probable cause hearing, the judge shall take cognizance of the evidence, if admissible, at the end of the in camera hearing without the questions being repeated or the evidence being resubmitted in open court.

Rule 413. Medical actions; statements to ameliorate or mitigate adverse outcome.

Statements by a health care provider apologizing for an adverse outcome in medical treatment, offers to undertake corrective or remedial treatment or actions, and gratuitous acts to assist affected persons shall not be admissible to prove negligence or culpable conduct by the health care provider in an action brought under Article 1B of Chapter 90 of the General Statutes.

Rule 414. Evidence of medical expenses.

Evidence offered to prove past medical expenses shall be limited to evidence of the amounts actually paid to satisfy the bills that have been satisfied, regardless of the source of payment, and evidence of the amounts actually necessary to satisfy the bills that have been incurred but not yet satisfied. This rule does not impose upon any party an affirmative duty to seek a reduction in billed charges to which the party is not contractually entitled.

Article 5. Privileges.

Rule 501. General rule.

Except as otherwise required by the Constitution of the United States, the privileges of a witness, person, government, state, or political subdivision thereof shall be determined in accordance with the law of this State.

Article 6. Witnesses.

Rule 601. General rule of competency; disqualification of witness.

(a) **General rule**. - Every person is competent to be a witness except as otherwise provided in these rules.

(b) **Disqualification of witness in general**. - A person is disqualified to testify as a witness when the court determines that the person is (1) incapable of expressing himself or herself concerning the matter as to be understood, either directly or through interpretation by one who can understand him or her, or (2) incapable of understanding the duty of a witness to tell the truth.

(c) **Disqualification of interested persons**. - Upon the trial of an action, or the hearing upon the merits of a special proceeding, a party or a person interested in the event, or a person from, through or under whom such a party or interested person derives his or her interest or title by assignment or otherwise, shall not be examined as a witness in his or her own behalf or interest, or in behalf of the party succeeding to his or her title or interest, against the executor, administrator or survivor of a deceased person, or the guardian of an incompetent person, or a person deriving his or her title or interest from, through or under a deceased or incompetent person by assignment or otherwise, concerning any oral communication between the witness and the deceased or incompetent person. However, this subdivision shall not apply when:

    (1) The executor, administrator, survivor, guardian, or person so deriving title or interest is examined in his or her own behalf regarding the subject matter of the oral communication.

    (2) The testimony of the deceased or incompetent person is given in evidence concerning the same transaction or communication.

    (3) Evidence of the subject matter of the oral communication is offered by the executor, administrator, survivor, guardian or person so deriving title or interest.

Nothing in this subdivision shall preclude testimony as to the identity of the operator of a motor vehicle in any case.

Rule 602. Lack of personal knowledge.

A witness may not testify to a matter unless evidence is introduced sufficient to support a finding that he has personal knowledge of the matter. Evidence to prove personal knowledge may, but need not, consist of the testimony of the witness himself. This rule is subject to the provisions of Rule 703, relating to opinion testimony by expert witnesses.

Rule 603. Oath or affirmation.

Before testifying, every witness shall be required to declare that he will testify truthfully, by oath or affirmation administered in a form calculated to awaken his conscience and impress his mind with his duty to do so.

Rule 604. Interpreters.

An interpreter is subject to the provisions of these rules relating to qualification as an expert and the administration of an oath or affirmation that he will make a true translation.

Rule 605. Competency of judge as witness.

The judge presiding at the trial may not testify in that trial as a witness. No objection need be made in order to preserve the point.

Rule 606. Competency of juror as witness.

(a) **At the trial**. - A member of the jury may not testify as a witness before that jury in the trial of the case in which he is sitting as a juror. If he is called so to testify, the opposing party shall be afforded an opportunity to object out of the presence of the jury.

(b) **Inquiry into validity of verdict or indictment**. - Upon an inquiry into the validity of a verdict or indictment, a juror may not testify as to any matter or statement occurring during the course of the jury's deliberations or to the effect of anything upon his or any other juror's mind or emotions as influencing him to assent to or dissent from the verdict or indictment or concerning his mental processes in connection therewith, except that a juror may testify on the question whether extraneous prejudicial information was improperly brought to the jury's attention or whether any outside influence was improperly brought to bear upon any juror. Nor may his affidavit or evidence of any statement by him concerning a matter about which he would be precluded from testifying be received for these purposes.

Rule 607. Who may impeach.

The credibility of a witness may be attacked by any party, including the party calling him.

Rule 608. Evidence of character and conduct of witness.

(a) **Opinion and reputation evidence of character**. - The credibility of a witness may be attacked or supported by evidence in the form of reputation or opinion as provided in Rule 405(a), but subject to these limitations: (1) the evidence may refer only to character for truthfulness or untruthfulness, and (2) evidence of truthful character is admissible only after the character of the witness for truthfulness has been attacked by opinion or reputation evidence or otherwise.

(b) **Specific instances of conduct**. - Specific instances of the conduct of a witness, for the purpose of attacking or supporting his credibility, other than conviction of crime as provided in Rule 609, may not be proved by extrinsic evidence. They may, however, in the discretion of the court, if probative of truthfulness or untruthfulness, be inquired into on cross-examination of the witness (1) concerning his character for truthfulness or untruthfulness, or (2) concerning the character for truthfulness or untruthfulness of another witness as to which character the witness being cross-examined has testified.

The giving of testimony, whether by an accused or by any other witness, does not operate as a waiver of his privilege against self-incrimination when examined with respect to matters which relate only to credibility.

Rule 609. Impeachment by evidence of conviction of crime.

(a) **General rule**. - For the purpose of attacking the credibility of a witness, evidence that the witness has been convicted of a felony, or of a Class A1, Class 1, or Class 2 misdemeanor, shall be admitted if elicited from the witness or established by public record during cross-examination or thereafter.

(b) **Time limit**. - Evidence of a conviction under this rule is not admissible if a period of more than 10 years has elapsed since the date of the conviction or of the release of the witness from the confinement imposed for that conviction, whichever is the later date, unless the court determines, in the interests of justice, that the probative value of the conviction supported by specific facts and circumstances substantially outweighs its prejudicial effect. However, evidence of a conviction more than 10 years old as calculated herein is not admissible unless the proponent gives to the adverse party sufficient advance written notice of intent to use such evidence to provide the adverse party with a fair opportunity to contest the use of such evidence.

(c) **Effect of pardon**. - Evidence of a conviction is not admissible under this rule if the conviction has been pardoned.

(d) **Juvenile adjudications**. - Evidence of juvenile adjudications is generally not admissible under this rule. The court may, however, in a criminal case allow evidence of a juvenile adjudication of a witness other than the accused if conviction of the offense would be admissible to attack the credibility of an adult and the court is satisfied that admission in evidence is necessary for a fair determination of the issue of guilt or innocence.

(e) **Pendency of appeal**. - The pendency of an appeal therefrom does not render evidence of a conviction inadmissible. Evidence of the pendency of an appeal is admissible.

Rule 610. Religious beliefs or opinions.

Evidence of the beliefs or opinions of a witness on matters of religion is not admissible for the purpose of showing that by reason of their nature his credibility is impaired or enhanced; provided, however, such evidence may be admitted for the purpose of showing interest or bias.

Rule 611. Mode and order of interrogation and presentation.

(a) **Control by court**. - The court shall exercise reasonable control over the mode and order of interrogating witnesses and presenting evidence so as to (1) make the interrogation and presentation effective for the ascertainment of the truth, (2) avoid needless consumption of time, and (3) protect witnesses from harassment or undue embarrassment.
(b) **Scope of cross-examination**. - A witness may be cross-examined on any matter relevant to any issue in the case, including credibility.
(c) **Leading questions**. - Leading questions should not be used on the direct examination of a witness except as may be necessary to develop his testimony. Ordinarily leading questions should be permitted on cross-examination. When a party calls a hostile witness, an adverse party, or a witness identified with an adverse party, interrogation may be by leading questions.

Rule 612. Writing or object used to refresh memory.

(a) **While testifying**. - If, while testifying, a witness uses a writing or object to refresh his memory, an adverse party is entitled to have the writing or object produced at the trial, hearing, or deposition in which the witness is testifying.
(b) **Before testifying**. - If, before testifying, a witness uses a writing or object to refresh his memory for the purpose of testifying and the court in its discretion determines that the interests of justice so require, an adverse party is entitled to have those portions of any writing or of the object which relate to the testimony produced, if practicable, at the trial, hearing, or deposition in which the witness is testifying.
(c) **Terms and conditions of production and use**. - A party entitled to have a writing or object produced under this rule is entitled to inspect it, to cross-examine the witness thereon, and to introduce in evidence those portions which relate to the testimony of the witness. If production of the writing or object at the trial, hearing, or deposition is impracticable, the court may order it made available for inspection. If it is claimed that the writing or object contains privileged information

or information not directly related to the subject matter of the testimony, the court shall examine the writing or object in camera, excise any such portions, and order delivery of the remainder to the party entitled thereto. Any portion withheld over objections shall be preserved and made available to the appellate court in the event of an appeal. If a writing or object is not produced, made available for inspection, or delivered pursuant to order under this rule, the court shall make any order justice requires, but in criminal cases if the prosecution elects not to comply, the order shall be one striking the testimony or, if justice so requires, declaring a mistrial.

Rule 613. Prior statements of witnesses.

In examining a witness concerning a prior statement made by him, whether written or not, the statement need not be shown nor its contents disclosed to him at that time, but on request the same shall be shown or disclosed to opposing counsel.

Rule 614. Calling and interrogation of witnesses by court.

(a) **Calling by court**. - The court may, on its own motion or at the suggestion of a party, call witnesses, and all parties are entitled to cross-examine witnesses thus called.

(b) **Interrogation by court**. - The court may interrogate witnesses, whether called by itself or by a party.

(c) **Objections**. - No objections are necessary with respect to the calling of a witness by the court or to questions propounded to a witness by the court but it shall be deemed that proper objection has been made and overruled.

Rule 615. Exclusion of witnesses.

At the request of a party the court may order witnesses excluded so that they cannot hear the testimony of other witnesses, and it may make the order of its own motion. This rule does not authorize exclusion of (1) a party who is a natural person, or (2) an officer or employee of a party that is not a natural person designated as its representative by its attorney, or (3) a person whose presence is shown by a party to be essential to the presentation of his cause, or (4) a person whose presence is determined by the court to be in the interest of justice.

Rule 616. Alternative testimony of witnesses with developmental disabilities or mental retardation in civil cases and special proceedings.

(a) **Definitions**. - The following definitions apply to this section:

(1) The definitions set out in G.S. 122C-3.

(2) "Remote testimony" means a method by which a witness testifies outside of an open forum and outside of the physical presence of a party or parties.

(b) **Remote Testimony Authorized**. - A person with a developmental disability or a person with mental retardation who is competent to testify may testify by remote testimony in a civil proceeding or special proceeding if the court determines by clear and convincing evidence that the witness would suffer serious emotional distress from testifying in the presence of a named party or parties or from testifying in an open forum and that the ability of the witness to communicate with the trier of fact would be impaired by testifying in the presence of a named party or parties or from testifying in an open forum.

(c) **Hearing Procedure**. - Upon motion of a party or the court's own motion, and for good cause shown, the court shall hold an evidentiary hearing to determine whether to allow remote testimony. The hearing shall be recorded unless recordation is waived by all parties. The presence of the witness is not required at the hearing unless so ordered by the presiding judge.

(d) **Order**. - An order allowing or disallowing the use of remote testimony shall state the findings and conclusions of law that support the court's determination. An order allowing the use of remote testimony also shall do all of the following:

(1) State the method by which the witness is to testify.

(2) List any individual or category of individuals allowed to be in or required to be excluded from the presence of the witness during testimony.

(3) State any special conditions necessary to facilitate the cross-examination of the witness.

(4) State any condition or limitation upon the participation of individuals in the presence of the witness during the testimony.

(5) State any other conditions necessary for taking or presenting testimony.

(e) **Testimony**. - The method of remote testimony shall allow the trier of fact and all parties to observe the demeanor of the witness as the witness testifies in a similar manner as if the witness were testifying in the open forum. Except as provided in this section, the court shall ensure that the counsel for all parties is physically present where the witness testifies and has a full and fair opportunity for examination and cross-examination of the witness. In a proceeding where a party is representing itself, the court may limit or deny the party from being physically present during testimony if the court finds that the witness would suffer serious emotional distress from testifying in the presence of the party. A party may waive the right to have counsel physically present where the witness testifies.

(f) **Nonexclusive Procedure and Standard**. - Nothing in this section shall prohibit the use or application of any other method or procedure authorized or required by law for the introduction into evidence of statements or testimony of a person with a developmental disability or a person with mental retardation.

Article 7. Opinions and Expert Testimony.

Rule 701. Opinion testimony by lay witness.

If the witness is not testifying as an expert, his testimony in the form of opinions or inferences is limited to those opinions or inferences which are (a) rationally based on the perception of the witness and (b) helpful to a clear understanding of his testimony or the determination of a fact in issue.

Rule 702. Testimony by experts.

(a) If scientific, technical or other specialized knowledge will assist the trier of fact to understand the evidence or to determine a fact in issue, a witness qualified as an expert by knowledge, skill, experience, training, or education, may testify thereto in the form of an opinion, or otherwise, if all of the following apply:
   (1) The testimony is based upon sufficient facts or data.
   (2) The testimony is the product of reliable principles and methods.
   (3) The witness has applied the principles and methods reliably to the facts of the case.
(a1) Notwithstanding any other provision of law, a witness may give expert testimony solely on the issue of impairment and not on the issue of specific alcohol concentration level relating to the following:
   (1) The results of a Horizontal Gaze Nystagmus (HGN) Test when the test is administered in accordance with the person's training by a person who has successfully completed training in HGN.
   (2) Whether a person was under the influence of one or more impairing substances, and the category of such impairing substance or substances, if the witness holds a current certification as a Drug Recognition Expert, issued by the State Department of Health and Human Services.
(b) In a medical malpractice action as defined in G.S. 90-21.11, a person shall not give expert testimony on the appropriate standard of health care as defined in G.S. 90-21.12 unless the person is a licensed health care provider in this State or another state and meets the following criteria:
   (1) If the party against whom or on whose behalf the testimony is offered is a specialist, the expert witness must:
      a. Specialize in the same specialty as the party against whom or on whose behalf the testimony is offered; or
      b. Specialize in a similar specialty which includes within its specialty the performance of the procedure that is the subject of the complaint and have prior experience treating similar patients.

(2) During the year immediately preceding the date of the occurrence that is the basis for the action, the expert witness must have devoted a majority of his or her professional time to either or both of the following:

   a. The active clinical practice of the same health profession in which the party against whom or on whose behalf the testimony is offered, and if that party is a specialist, the active clinical practice of the same specialty or a similar specialty which includes within its specialty the performance of the procedure that is the subject of the complaint and have prior experience treating similar patients; or

   b. The instruction of students in an accredited health professional school or accredited residency or clinical research program in the same health profession in which the party against whom or on whose behalf the testimony is offered, and if that party is a specialist, an accredited health professional school or accredited residency or clinical research program in the same specialty.

(c) Notwithstanding subsection (b) of this section, if the party against whom or on whose behalf the testimony is offered is a general practitioner, the expert witness, during the year immediately preceding the date of the occurrence that is the basis for the action, must have devoted a majority of his or her professional time to either or both of the following:

   (1) Active clinical practice as a general practitioner; or

   (2) Instruction of students in an accredited health professional school or accredited residency or clinical research program in the general practice of medicine.

(d) Notwithstanding subsection (b) of this section, a physician who qualifies as an expert under subsection (a) of this Rule and who by reason of active clinical practice or instruction of students has knowledge of the applicable standard of care for nurses, nurse practitioners, certified registered nurse anesthetists, certified registered nurse midwives, physician assistants, or other medical support staff may give expert testimony in a medical malpractice action with respect to the standard of care of which he is knowledgeable of nurses, nurse practitioners, certified registered nurse anesthetists, certified registered nurse midwives, physician assistants licensed under Chapter 90 of the General Statutes, or other medical support staff.

(e) Upon motion by either party, a resident judge of the superior court in the county or judicial district in which the action is pending may allow expert testimony on the appropriate standard of health care by a witness who does not meet the requirements of subsection (b) or (c) of this Rule, but who is otherwise qualified as an expert witness, upon a showing by the movant of extraordinary circumstances and a determination by the court that the motion should be allowed to serve the ends of justice.

(f) In an action alleging medical malpractice, an expert witness shall not testify on a contingency fee basis.

(g) This section does not limit the power of the trial court to disqualify an expert witness on grounds other than the qualifications set forth in this section.

(h) Notwithstanding subsection (b) of this section, in a medical malpractice action as defined in G.S. 90-21.11(2)b. against a hospital, or other health care or medical facility, a person shall not give expert testimony on the appropriate standard of care as to administrative or other nonclinical issues unless the person has substantial knowledge, by virtue of his or her training and experience, about the standard of care among hospitals, or health care or medical facilities, of the same type as the hospital, or health care or medical facility, whose actions or inactions are the subject of the testimony situated in the same or similar communities at the time of the alleged act giving rise to the cause of action.

(i) A witness qualified as an expert in accident reconstruction who has performed a reconstruction of a crash, or has reviewed the report of investigation, with proper foundation may give an opinion as to the speed of a vehicle even if the witness did not observe the vehicle moving.

Rule 703. Bases of opinion testimony by experts.

The facts or data in the particular case upon which an expert bases an opinion or inference may be those perceived by or made known to him at or before the hearing. If of a type reasonably relied upon by experts in the particular field in forming opinions or inferences upon the subject, the facts or data need not be admissible in evidence.

Rule 704. Opinion on ultimate issue.

Testimony in the form of an opinion or inference is not objectionable because it embraces an ultimate issue to be decided by the trier of fact.

Rule 705. Disclosure of facts or data underlying expert opinion.

The expert may testify in terms of opinion or inference and give his reasons therefor without prior disclosure of the underlying facts or data, unless an adverse party requests otherwise, in which event the expert will be required to disclose such underlying facts or data on direct examination or voir dire before stating the opinion. The expert may in any event be required to disclose the underlying facts or data on cross-examination.

There shall be no requirement that expert testimony be in response to a hypothetical question.

Rule 706. Court appointed experts.

(a) **Appointment**. - The court may on its own motion or on the motion of any party enter an order to show cause why expert witnesses should not be appointed, and may request the parties to submit nominations. The court may appoint any expert witnesses agreed upon by the parties, and may appoint witnesses of its own selection. An expert witness shall not be appointed by the court unless he consents to act. A witness so appointed shall be informed of his duties by the court in writing, a copy of which shall be filed with the clerk, or at a conference in which the parties shall have opportunity to participate. A witness so appointed shall advise the parties of his findings, if any; his deposition may be taken by any party; and he may be called to testify by the court or any party. He shall be subject to cross-examination by each party, including a party calling him as a witness.

(b) **Compensation**. - Expert witnesses so appointed are entitled to reasonable compensation in whatever sum the court may allow. The compensation thus fixed is payable from funds which may be provided by law in criminal cases and civil actions and proceedings involving just compensation for the taking of property. In other civil actions and proceedings the compensation shall be paid by the parties in such proportion and at such time as the court directs, and thereafter charged in like manner as other costs.

(c) **Disclosure of appointment**. - In the exercise of its discretion, the court may authorize disclosure to the jury of the fact that the court appointed the expert witness.

(d) **Parties' experts of own selection**. - Nothing in this rule limits the parties in calling expert witnesses of their own selection.

Article 8. Hearsay.

Rule 801. Definitions and exception for admissions of a party-opponent.

The following definitions apply under this Article:

(a) **Statement**. - A "statement" is (1) an oral or written assertion or (2) nonverbal conduct of a person, if it is intended by him as an assertion.

(b) **Declarant**. - A "declarant" is a person who makes a statement.

(c) **Hearsay**. - "Hearsay" is a statement, other than one made by the declarant while testifying at the trial or hearing, offered in evidence to prove the truth of the matter asserted.

(d) **Exception for Admissions by a Party-Opponent**. - A statement is admissible as an exception to the hearsay rule if it is offered against a party and it is (A) his own statement, in either his individual or a representative capacity, or (B) a statement of which he has manifested his adoption or belief in its truth, or (C) a statement by a person authorized by him to make a statement concerning the subject, or (D) a statement by his agent or servant concerning a matter within the scope of his agency or employment, made during the existence of the relationship or (E) a statement by a coconspirator of such party during the course and in furtherance of the conspiracy.

Rule 802. Hearsay rule.

Hearsay is not admissible except as provided by statute or by these rules.

Rule 803. Hearsay exceptions; availability of declarant immaterial.

The following are not excluded by the hearsay rule, even though the declarant is available as a witness:

(1) **Present Sense Impression**. - A statement describing or explaining an event or condition made while the declarant was perceiving the event or condition, or immediately thereafter.

(2) **Excited Utterance**. - A statement relating to a startling event or condition made while the declarant was under the stress of excitement caused by the event or condition.

(3) **Then Existing Mental, Emotional, or Physical Condition**. - A statement of the declarant's then existing state of mind, emotion, sensation, or physical condition (such as intent, plan, motive, design, mental feeling, pain, and bodily health), but not including a statement of memory or belief to prove the fact remembered or believed unless it relates to the execution, revocation, identification, or terms of declarant's will.

(4) **Statements for Purposes of Medical Diagnosis or Treatment**. - Statements made for purposes of medical diagnosis or treatment and describing medical history, or past or present symptoms, pain, or sensations, or the inception or general character of the cause or external source thereof insofar as reasonably pertinent to diagnosis or treatment.

(5) **Recorded Recollection**. - A memorandum or record concerning a matter about which a witness once had knowledge but now has insufficient recollection to enable him to testify fully and accurately, shown to have been made or adopted by the witness when the matter was fresh in his memory and to reflect that knowledge correctly. If admitted, the memorandum or record may be read into evidence but may not itself be received as an exhibit unless offered by an adverse party.

(6) **Records of Regularly Conducted Activity**. - A memorandum, report, record, or data compilation, in any form, of acts, events, conditions, opinions, or diagnoses, made at or near the time by, or from information transmitted by, a person with knowledge, if (i) kept in the course of a regularly conducted business activity and (ii) it was the regular practice of that business activity to make the memorandum, report, record, or data compilation, all as shown by the testimony of the custodian or other qualified witness, or by affidavit or by document under seal under Rule 902 of the Rules of Evidence made by the custodian or witness, unless the source of information or the method or circumstances of preparation indicate lack of trustworthiness. Authentication of evidence by affidavit shall be confined to the records of nonparties, and the proponent of that evidence shall give advance notice to all other parties of intent to offer the evidence with authentication by affidavit. The term "business" as used in this paragraph includes business, institution, association, profession, occupation, and calling of every kind, whether or not conducted for profit.

(7) **Absence of Entry in Records Kept in Accordance with the Provisions of Paragraph (6)**. - Evidence that a matter is not included in the memoranda, reports, records, or data compilations, in any form, kept in accordance with the provisions of paragraph (6), to prove the nonoccurrence or nonexistence of the matter, if the matter was of a kind of which a memorandum, report, record, or data compilation was regularly made and preserved, unless the sources of information or other circumstances indicate lack of trustworthiness.

(8) **Public Records and Reports**. - Records, reports, statements, or data compilations, in any form, of public offices or agencies, setting forth (A) the activities of the office or agency, or (B) matters observed pursuant to duty imposed by law as to which

matters there was a duty to report, excluding, however, in criminal cases matters observed by police officers and other law-enforcement personnel, or (C) in civil actions and proceedings and against the State in criminal cases, factual findings resulting from an investigation made pursuant to authority granted by law, unless the sources of information or other circumstances indicate lack of trustworthiness.

(9) **Records of Vital Statistics**. - Records or data compilations, in any form, of births, fetal deaths, deaths, or marriages, if the report thereof was made to a public office pursuant to requirements of law.

(10) **Absence of Public Record or Entry**. - To prove the absence of a record, report, statement, or data compilation, in any form, or the nonoccurrence or nonexistence of a matter of which a record, report, statement, or data compilation, in any form, was regularly made and preserved by a public office or agency, evidence in the form of a certification in accordance with Rule 902, or testimony, that diligent search failed to disclose the record, report, statement, or data compilation, or entry.

(11) **Records of Religious Organizations**. - Statements of births, marriages, divorces, deaths, legitimacy, ancestry, relationship by blood or marriage, or other similar facts of personal or family history, contained in a regularly kept record of a religious organization.

(12) **Marriage, Baptismal, and Similar Certificates**. - Statements of fact contained in a certificate that the maker performed a marriage or other ceremony or administered a sacrament, made by a clergyman, public official, or other person authorized by the rules or practices of a religious organization or by law to perform the act certified, and purporting to have been issued at the time of the act or within a reasonable time thereafter.

(13) **Family Records**. - Statements of fact concerning personal or family history contained in family Bibles, genealogies, charts, engravings on rings, inscriptions on family portraits, engravings on urns, crypts, or tombstones, or the like.

(14) **Records of Documents Affecting an Interest in Property**. - The record of a document purporting to establish or affect an interest in property, as proof of the content of the original recorded document and its execution and delivery by each person by whom it purports to have been executed, if the record is a record of a public office and an applicable statute authorizes the recording of documents of that kind in that office.

(15) **Statements in Documents Affecting an Interest in Property**. - A statement contained in a document purporting to establish or affect an interest in property if the matter stated was relevant to

the purpose of the document, unless dealings with the property since the document was made have been inconsistent with the truth of the statement or the purport of the document.

(16) **Statements in Ancient Documents**. - Statements in a document in existence 20 years or more the authenticity of which is established.

(17) **Market Reports, Commercial Publications**. - Market quotations, tabulations, lists, directories, or other published compilations, generally used and relied upon by the public or by persons in particular occupations.

(18) **Learned Treatises**. - To the extent called to the attention of an expert witness upon cross-examination or relied upon by him in direct examination, statements contained in published treatises, periodicals, or pamphlets on a subject of history, medicine, or other science or art, established as a reliable authority by the testimony or admission of the witness or by other expert testimony or by judicial notice. If admitted, the statements may be read into evidence but may not be received as exhibits.

(19) **Reputation Concerning Personal or Family History**. - Reputation among members of his family by blood, adoption, or marriage, or among his associates, or in the community, concerning a person's birth, adoption, marriage, divorce, death, legitimacy, relationship by blood, adoption, or marriage, ancestry, or other similar fact of his personal or family history.

(20) **Reputation Concerning Boundaries or General History**. - Reputation in a community, arising before the controversy, as to boundaries of or customs affecting lands in the community, and reputation as to events of general history important to the community or state or nation in which located.

(21) **Reputation as to Character**. - Reputation of a person's character among his associates or in the community.

(22) (Reserved).

(23) **Judgment as to Personal, Family or General History, or Boundaries**. - Judgments as proof of matters of personal, family or general history, or boundaries, essential to the judgment, if the same would be provable by evidence of reputation.

(24) **Other Exceptions**. - A statement not specifically covered by any of the foregoing exceptions but having equivalent circumstantial guarantees of trustworthiness, if the court determines that (A) the statement is offered as evidence of a material fact; (B) the statement is more probative on the point for which it is offered than any other evidence which the proponent can procure through reasonable efforts; and (C) the general purposes of these rules and the interests of justice will best be served by admission of the statement into evidence. However, a statement may not be

admitted under this exception unless the proponent of it gives written notice stating his intention to offer the statement and the particulars of it, including the name and address of the declarant, to the adverse party sufficiently in advance of offering the statement to provide the adverse party with a fair opportunity to prepare to meet the statement.

Rule 804. Hearsay exceptions; declarant unavailable.

(a) **Definition of unavailability**. - "Unavailability as a witness" includes situations in which the declarant:
  (1) Is exempted by ruling of the court on the ground of privilege from testifying concerning the subject matter of his statement; or
  (2) Persists in refusing to testify concerning the subject matter of his statement despite an order of the court to do so; or
  (3) Testifies to a lack of memory of the subject matter of his statement; or
  (4) Is unable to be present or to testify at the hearing because of death or then existing physical or mental illness or infirmity; or
  (5) Is absent from the hearing and the proponent of his statement has been unable to procure his attendance (or in the case of a hearsay exception under subdivision (b)(2), (3), or (4), his attendance or testimony) by process or other reasonable means.
  A declarant is not unavailable as a witness if his exemption, refusal, claim of lack of memory, inability, or absence is due to the procurement or wrongdoing of the proponent of his statement for the purpose of preventing the witness from attending or testifying.

(b) **Hearsay exceptions**. - The following are not excluded by the hearsay rule if the declarant is unavailable as a witness:
  (1) Former Testimony. - Testimony given as a witness at another hearing of the same or a different proceeding, or in a deposition taken in compliance with law in the course of the same or another proceeding, if the party against whom the testimony is now offered, or, in a civil action or proceeding, a predecessor in interest, had an opportunity and similar motive to develop the testimony by direct, cross, or redirect examination.
  (2) Statement Under Belief of Impending Death. - A statement made by a declarant while believing that his death was imminent, concerning the cause or circumstances of what he believed to be his impending death.
  (3) Statement Against Interest. - A statement which was at the time of its making so far contrary to the declarant's pecuniary or proprietary interest, or so far tended to subject him to civil or criminal liability, or to render invalid a claim by him against another, that a reasonable man in his position would not have

made the statement unless he believed it to be true. A statement tending to expose the declarant to criminal liability is not admissible in a criminal case unless corroborating circumstances clearly indicate the trustworthiness of the statement.

(4) Statement of Personal or Family History. - (A) A statement concerning the declarant's own birth, adoption, marriage, divorce, legitimacy, relationship by blood, adoption, or marriage, ancestry, or other similar fact of personal or family history, even though declarant had no means of acquiring personal knowledge of the matter stated; or (B) a statement concerning the foregoing matters, and death also, of another person, if the declarant was related to the other by blood, adoption, or marriage or was so intimately associated with the other's family as to be likely to have accurate information concerning the matter declared.

(5) Other Exceptions. - A statement not specifically covered by any of the foregoing exceptions but having equivalent circumstantial guarantees of trustworthiness, if the court determines that (A) the statement is offered as evidence of a material fact; (B) the statement is more probative on the point for which it is offered than any other evidence which the proponent can procure through reasonable efforts; and (C) the general purposes of these rules and the interests of justice will best be served by admission of the statement into evidence. However, a statement may not be admitted under this exception unless the proponent of it gives written notice stating his intention to offer the statement and the particulars of it, including the name and address of the declarant, to the adverse party sufficiently in advance of offering the statement to provide the adverse party with a fair opportunity to prepare to meet the statement.

Rule 805. Hearsay within hearsay.

Hearsay included within hearsay is not excluded under the hearsay rule if each part of the combined statements conforms with an exception to the hearsay rule provided in these rules.

Rule 806. Attacking and supporting credibility of declarant.

When a hearsay statement has been admitted in evidence, the credibility of the declarant may be attacked, and if attacked may be supported, by any evidence which would be admissible for those purposes if declarant had testified as a witness. Evidence of a statement or conduct by the declarant at any time, inconsistent with his hearsay statement, is not subject to any requirement that he may have been afforded an opportunity to deny or explain. If the party against whom a hearsay statement has been admitted calls the declarant as a witness, the party is entitled to examine him on the statement as if under cross-examination.

Article 9. Authentication and Identification.

Rule 901. Requirement of authentication or identification.

(a) **General provision**. - The requirement of authentication or identification as a condition precedent to admissibility is satisfied by evidence sufficient to support a finding that the matter in question is what its proponent claims.

(b) **Illustrations**. - By way of illustration only, and not by way of limitation, the following are examples of authentication or identification conforming with the requirements of this rule:

    (1) Testimony of Witness with Knowledge. - Testimony that a matter is what it is claimed to be.

    (2) Nonexpert Opinion on Handwriting. - Nonexpert opinion as to the genuineness of handwriting, based upon familiarity not acquired for purposes of the litigation.

    (3) Comparison by Trier or Expert Witness. - Comparison by the trier of fact or by expert witnesses with specimens which have been authenticated.

    (4) Distinctive Characteristics and the Like. - Appearance, contents, substance, internal patterns, or other distinctive characteristics, taken in conjunction with circumstances.

    (5) Voice Identification. - Identification of a voice, whether heard firsthand or through mechanical or electronic transmission or recording, by opinion based upon hearing the voice at any time under circumstances connecting it with the alleged speaker.

    (6) Telephone Conversations. - Telephone conversations, by evidence that a call was made to the number assigned at the time by the telephone company to a particular person or business, if (A) in the case of a person, circumstances, including self-identification, show the person answering to be the one called, or (B) in the case of a business, the call was made to a place of business and the conversation related to business reasonably transacted over the telephone.

    (7) Public Records or Reports. - Evidence that a writing authorized by law to be recorded or filed and in fact recorded or filed in a public office, or a purported public record, report, statement, or data compilation, in any form, is from the public office where items of this nature are kept.

    (8) Ancient Documents or Data Compilations. - Evidence that a document or data compilation, in any form, (A) is in such condition as to create no suspicion concerning its authenticity, (B) was in a place where it, if authentic, would likely be, and (C) has been in existence 20 years or more at the time it is offered.

(9) Process or System. - Evidence describing a process or system used to produce a result and showing that the process or system produces an accurate result.

(10) Methods Provided by Statute. - Any method of authentication or identification provided by statute.

Rule 902. Self-authentication.

Extrinsic evidence of authenticity as a condition precedent to admissibility is not required with respect to the following:

(1) **Domestic Public Documents Under Seal**. - A document bearing a seal purporting to be that of the United States, or of any state, district, commonwealth, territory or insular possession thereof, or the Trust Territory of the Pacific Islands, or of a political subdivision, department, officer, or agency thereof, and a signature purporting to be an attestation or execution.

(2) **Domestic Public Documents Not Under Seal**. - A document purporting to bear the signature in his official capacity of an officer or employee of any entity included in paragraph (1) hereof, having no seal, if a public officer having a seal and having official duties in the district or political subdivision of the officer or employee certifies under seal that the signer has the official capacity and that the signature is genuine.

(3) **Foreign Public Documents**. - A document purporting to be executed or attested in his official capacity by a person authorized by the laws of a foreign country to make the execution or attestation, and accompanied by a final certification as to the genuineness of the signature and official position (A) of the executing or attesting person, or (B) of any foreign official whose certificate of genuineness of signature and official position relates to the execution or attestation or is in a chain of certificates of genuineness of signature and official position relating to the execution or attestation. A final certification may be made by a secretary of embassy or legation, consul general, consul, vice consul, or consular agent of the United States, or a diplomatic or consular official of the foreign country assigned or accredited to the United States. If reasonable opportunity has been given to all parties to investigate the authenticity and accuracy of official documents, the court may, for good cause shown, order that they be treated as presumptively authentic without final certification or permit them to be evidenced by an attested summary with or without final certification.

(4) **Certified Copies of Public Records**. - A copy of an official record or report or entry therein, or of a document authorized by law to be recorded or filed and actually recorded or filed in a

public office, including data compilations in any form, certified as correct by the custodian or other person authorized to make the certification, by certificate complying with paragraph (1), (2), or (3) or complying with any law of the United States or of this State.

(5) **Official Publications**. - Books, pamphlets, or other publications purporting to be issued by public authority.

(6) **Newspapers and Periodicals**. - Printed materials purporting to be newspapers or periodicals.

(7) **Trade Inscriptions and the Like**. - Inscriptions, signs, tags, or labels purporting to have been affixed in the course of business and indicating ownership, control, or origin.

(8) **Acknowledged Documents**. - Documents accompanied by a certificate of acknowledgment executed in the manner provided by law by a notary public or other officer authorized by law to take acknowledgments.

(9) **Commercial Paper and Related Documents**. - Commercial paper, signatures thereon, and documents relating thereto to the extent provided by general commercial law.

(10) **Presumptions Created by Law**. - Any signature, document, or other matter declared by any law of the United States or of this State to be presumptively or prima facie genuine or authentic.

Rule 903. Subscribing witness' testimony unnecessary.

The testimony of a subscribing witness is not necessary to authenticate a writing unless required by the laws of the jurisdiction whose laws govern the validity of the writing.

Article 10. Contents of Writings, Recordings and Photographs.

Rule 1001. Definitions.

For the purposes of this Article the following definitions are applicable:

(1) **Writings and Recordings**. - "Writings" and "recordings" consist of letters, words, sounds, or numbers, or their equivalent, set down by handwriting, typewriting, printing, photostating, photographing, magnetic impulse, mechanical or electronic recording, or other form of data compilation.

(2) **Photographs**. - "Photographs" include still photographs, x-ray films, video tapes, and motion pictures.

(3) **Original**. - An "original" of a writing or recording is the writing or recording itself or any counterpart intended to have the same effect by a person executing or issuing it. An "original" of a photograph includes the negative or any print therefrom. If data are stored in a computer or similar device, any printout or other output readable by sight, shown to reflect the data accurately, is an "original."

(4) **Duplicate**. - A "duplicate" is a counterpart produced by the same impression as the original, or from the same matrix, or by means of photography, including enlargements and miniatures, or by mechanical or electronic re-recording, or by chemical reproduction, or by other equivalent techniques which accurately reproduce the original.

Rule 1002. Requirement of original.

To prove the content of a writing, recording, or photograph, the original writing, recording, or photograph is required, except as otherwise provided in these rules or by statute.

Rule 1003. Admissibility of duplicates.

A duplicate is admissible to the same extent as an original unless (1) a genuine question is raised as to the authenticity of the original or (2) in the circumstances it would be unfair to admit the duplicate in lieu of the original.

Rule 1004. Admissibility of other evidence of contents.

The original is not required, and other evidence of the contents of a writing, recording, or photograph is admissible if:

(1) **Originals Lost or Destroyed**. - All originals are lost or have been destroyed, unless the proponent lost or destroyed them in bad faith; or

(2) **Original Not Obtainable**. - No original can be obtained by any available judicial process or procedure; or

(3) **Original in Possession of Opponent**. - At a time when an original was under the control of a party against whom offered, he was put on notice, by the pleadings or otherwise, that the contents would be a subject of proof at the hearing, and he does not produce the original at the hearing; or

(4) **Collateral Matters**. - The writing, recording, or photograph is not closely related to a controlling issue.

Rule 1005. Public records.

The contents of an official record, or of a document authorized to be recorded or filed and actually recorded or filed, including data compilations in any form, if otherwise admissible, may be proved by copy, certified as correct in accordance with Rule 902 or testified to be correct by a witness who has compared it with the original. If a copy which complies with the foregoing cannot be obtained by the exercise of reasonable diligence, then other evidence of the contents may be given.

Rule 1006. Summaries.

The contents of voluminous writings, recordings, or photographs which cannot conveniently be examined in court may be presented in the form of a chart, summary, or calculation. The originals, or duplicates, shall be made available for examination or copying, or both, by other parties at a reasonable time and place. The court may order that they be produced in court.

Rule 1007. Testimony or written admission of party.

Contents of writings, recordings, or photographs may be proved by the testimony or deposition of the party against whom offered or by his written admission, without accounting for the nonproduction of the original.

Rule 1008. Functions of court and jury.

When the admissibility of other evidence of contents of writings, recordings, or photographs under these rules depends upon the fulfillment of a condition of fact, the question whether the condition has been fulfilled is ordinarily for the court to determine in accordance with the provisions of Rule 104. However, when an issue is raised (a) whether the asserted writing ever existed, or (b) whether another writing, recording, or photograph produced at the trial is the original, or (c) whether other evidence of contents correctly reflects the contents, the issue is for the trier of fact to determine as in the case of other issues of fact.

Article 11. Miscellaneous Rules.

Rule 1101. Applicability of rules.

(a) **Proceedings generally**. - Except as otherwise provided in subdivision (b) or by statute, these rules apply to all actions and proceedings in the courts of this State.

(b) **Rules inapplicable**. - The rules other than those with respect to privileges do not apply in the following situations:

　(1) Preliminary Questions of Fact. - The determination of questions of fact preliminary to admissibility of evidence when the issue is to be determined by the court under Rule 104(a).

　(2) Grand Jury. - Proceedings before grand juries.

　(3) Miscellaneous Proceedings. - Proceedings for extradition or rendition; first appearance before district court judge or probable cause hearing in criminal cases; sentencing, or granting or revoking probation; issuance of warrants for arrest, criminal summonses, and search warrants; proceedings with respect to release on bail or otherwise.

　(4) Contempt Proceedings. - Contempt proceedings in which the court is authorized by law to act summarily.

Rule 1102. Short title.

These rules shall be known and may be cited as the "North Carolina Rules of Evidence."

www.ingramcontent.com/pod-product-compliance
Lightning Source LLC
Chambersburg PA
CBHW060514220326
41598CB00025B/3654